NATIONAL GEOGRAPHIC

D0503686

PASSPORT TO WONDER

PATHFINDER EDITION

By Marylou Tousignant

CONTENTS

PASSPORT to WONDER

By Marylou Tousignant

What are the most amazing things people have ever built? Could you choose just seven?

THAT'S WHAT the ancient Greeks did more than 2,000 years ago. Their list is called the Seven Wonders of the Ancient World. Unfortunately, only one ancient wonder still stands today—the Pyramids of Giza in Egypt. Nature and humans destroyed the other six.

One day, however, a Swiss adventurer thought it was time for a new list. He began a campaign to get people excited about protecting the world's treasures, and he asked people to vote for their favorites.

Now it's your turn. Get ready to trek across four continents to visit the New 7 Wonders of the World. As you visit each site, ask yourself this question: Did the voters get it right?

Labor of Love

First stop: Agra, India.

You peer up at the giant stone dome of the Taj Mahal (left). It glistens pink and tangerine at dawn, a glowing gift to the world.

Yet this palace is really a tomb. In fact, it is a ruler's gift to his wife. According to the legend, before dying, she asked for a **monument** to their love. The broken-hearted ruler spent a fortune building the Taj Mahal, where he finally buried his beloved.

The job took more than 20,000 workers and 1,000 elephants, which were used to haul giant blocks of white marble. Finally, in the 1650s, after more than 20 years of construction, it was complete.

Today, the Taj Mahal still shines. Its 73 meter (240 foot) dome still shimmers in the moonlight. Some people think it is the most beautiful building in the world. What do you think?

ASIA
INDIA
INDIAN OCEAN

Winding Wall

Next stop: northern China.

You're on top of an enormous brick wall that seems to wind on forever in both directions. Of course, this serpentine giant isn't just any wall—it's the Great Wall of China.

The Chinese began building walls more than 3,000 years ago. Their purpose was to keep enemies out. Most of the Great Wall standing today was built during the Ming dynasty, a stable, influential ruling period that lasted from 1368 to 1644.

Today, the Great Wall remains the largest human-made **structure** in the world. A recent study found that it stretches more than 8,850 kilometers (almost 5,500 miles), twice the width of the United States! Trekkers and adventures alike are drawn to this giant brick and stone path, which snakes over mountains, crosses deserts, and wanders through the Chinese countryside on an endless journey to the sea.

Near China's **capital**, Beijing, the wall is 7.6 meters (25 feet) high. In other places, no wall remains. Sand, storms, and earthquakes have damaged it. People have taken bricks as souvenirs or to build homes. To help China save this treasure, now you can take only photos.

Smoke Signals. *Watchtowers along the Great Wall served as shelters for guards. They used smoke from fires for communication.*

Rock City

You've got one more stop in Asia: the country of Jordan.

You ride a camel through a canyon in southwest Jordan as rose-colored cliff walls rise high above you. The canyon is so narrow that in places it's hard for two camels to squeeze past one another.

Suddenly, you come to an opening. The cliffs are no longer cliffs—they are city buildings. Are your eyes fooling you? No. You're standing in hot, dusty Petra. *Petra* is Greek for "rock." People carved Petra out of sheer cliffs of pink sandstone. Look up. Some carvings are as tall as ten-story buildings!

About 2,000 years ago, Petra thrived as a busy marketplace with a population of as many as 30,000 people. The smell of spices, perfumes, and camels filled the air. People showed off their riches and built fancy houses and tombs.

Then, in the fourth century, an earthquake destroyed half of Petra. In time, people left and the city was forgotten.

In the early 1800s, an explorer found the **ruins** of Petra. Scientists have been digging out its treasures ever since. Watch where you step! Three-fourths of the city remains buried underground.

EUROPE
ITALY

Beastly Battles

Now you're off to Europe. Next stop: Rome, Italy.

Evening traffic zooms behind you as you stand on a sidewalk and stare up 48 meters (159 feet) at a crumbling stone stadium. It's the Roman Colosseum.

Fire and earthquakes have damaged this giant building, and huge chunks are missing. You begin to see the night sky through its many arches.

Close your eyes. Imagine the roar of a cheering crowd. When it opened in 80 C.E., the Colosseum was the main place to go for fun. The stadium held 50,000 people, who applauded and cheered as fighters called gladiators fought to the death.

Sometimes, the Romans filled the arena with water deep enough for real ships, and battles between gladiators took place aboard them. When the arena was dry, lions, bears, and even elephants sprang up from trap doors in the floor to test the gladiators' skills.

These beastly battles finally were outlawed in 523 C.E., and the Colosseum closed soon after. Today, only untamed cats and tourists like you roam the arena.

Slithering Snakes

It's time to head to the Americas. Your first stop: the ruins of Chichén Itzá in southern Mexico.

The Maya and Toltec people lived here between the 7th and 13th centuries. They were expert mathematicians, and they used their knowledge to build huge stone temples and pyramids. They also studied the stars. How talented were they? Take a close look at their famous pyramid, the Temple of Kukulkán.

Watch closely. Did you just see that snake-like shadow slither down its steps? The sun cast this wild shadow. The snake emerges on the equinoxes, or the first days of spring and fall. It is one way the people paid tribute to their serpent god, Quezalcóatl. The moving shadow also helped them keep track of the passage of time.

Yearly Steps. *The pyramid of Kukulkán (El Castillo, or "The Castle") has 91 steps on each side, plus one on top. That adds up to 365 steps, one for each day of the year.*

PERU ★
PACIFIC
OCEAN

Llama Landscape. *Machu Picchu means "ancient mountain peak" in the Inca language. Llamas like the one in this photo live in the mountains surrounding the city.*

Cloud City

Next stop: Peru.

How do you get to a city in the clouds? You could take a high-speed train, but you decide to use foot power instead. First, you hike four days through the Andes Mountains. You reach a narrow ridge 2,350 meters (7,700 feet) above sea level. The peaks here are so steep that you wonder if you might slide right off.

That's when you come upon the ruins of an ancient city. Its beautiful stone buildings seem to cling to the high green slopes. You've reached Machu Picchu. This city is sometimes called "the lost city of the Inca." The Inca were a rich and powerful people who, by the end of the 1400s, ruled a large part of western South America.

No one is certain why or how the Inca built this city in such a rugged landscape—they did not leave a written record. But experts believe that Machu Picchu was a vacation spot for Inca rulers.

Check out the elegant houses, temples, and tombs. The hand-carved granite blocks fit together so tightly that you can't even slip a knife blade between them. Can you imagine some of these buildings covered in gold? They may once have been!

1 RL

SHARJAH
4 DEPENDENCIES AIR MAIL

Welcoming Arms

Your last stop: Rio de Janeiro, Brazil. Tired of hiking? Take the train this time. It winds through a tunnel of trees in the world's largest city forest. Then it climbs Corcovado Mountain, a peak that rises 704 meters (2,310 feet) above sea level. The view from the top takes your breath away. The Atlantic Ocean sparkles in the distance as the huge city spreads beneath your feet.

Look up. You see a huge statue. The statue weighs 700 tons, stands 38 meters (125 feet) tall, and its open arms stretch 28 meters (92 feet) wide.

In 1931, the people of Brazil gave the statue to themselves as a gift. It celebrated one hundred years of independence from Portugal. Today, it's a symbol of Brazil's warm and welcoming culture.

The statue is made of concrete and soapstone, making it both strong and easy to carve. In 2008, lightning struck the statue. Luckily, it didn't cause any major damage, but it did give quite a show!

City View. *Visitors must climb more than 200 steps to reach the base of the giant statue, where they are rewarded with a great view of the city of Rio de Janeiro.*

Wonder Why

It's time to go back home and consider the winners. Are the New 7 Wonders big enough, beautiful enough, "Wow!" enough?

People have built many cool things that didn't make the final list. For example, voters did not pick the Statue of Liberty in New York City. They skipped France's Eiffel Tower. No places in Africa or Australia won.

So think: What places would make your list of Wonders? You just might have to pack your passport and go explore!

WORDWISE

capital: city where the government of a country or state is located

monument: a famous place or building that celebrates a person, event, or idea

ruin: the remaining pieces of something

structure: a building or space that is made by people

MORE WONDERS

1. Crowning Touch.
A 168-step spiral staircase leads to the Statue of Liberty's crown. The view? New York Harbor, once a first stop for many immigrants to the United States.

2. Keeping Watch.
Why do hundreds of giant heads and torsos dot Chile's remote Easter Island? Most have their backs to the sea. No one is sure why.

NORTH AMERICA

ATLANTIC OCEAN

1

4

5

6

PACIFIC OCEAN

SOUTH AMERICA

2

3. Ancient Wonder.
The largest pyramid ever built is near Giza, Egypt. Pharaoh Khufu was buried here. So was a 4,600-year-old boat, maybe to take him to his afterlife.

4. World Welcome.
The Eiffel Tower was built to greet visitors to the 1889 World's Fair in Paris, France. Critics called the steel tower "monstrous." Not anymore!

IN 2007, millions of people voted for the New 7 Wonders of the World. When the votes were tallied, 14 finalists didn't make the cut. See if you recognize any of these wonderful runners-up.

8. Terrific Temple.
Angkor, Cambodia, is called "the city of temples." The most famous is Angkor Wat. Its tower is a symbol of Mount Meru, the Hindu gods' mythical home.

7. Sidney Sings.
How many tiles cover this roof shaped like soaring sails? More than one million! Inside the Sydney Opera House in Australia, it's the voices that soar.

5. Fantastic Fort.
It's clear why the Alhambra, in Spain, means "red fort" in Arabic. Inside its clay walls, visitors find colorful tiles, fountains, and carved Arabic verses.

6. Desert Jewel.
Long ago, Timbuktu was called "the city of gold," yet this African city's true treasure is knowledge. Thousands once studied at the Sankore mosque shown here.

WONDERFUL
WORLD

Retrace your steps. Answer these questions about the New 7 Wonders of the World.

1 Why does the author call the Taj Mahal a "labor of love"?

2 *Petra* is the Greek word for "rock." Why is this a good name for the city of Petra?

3 Name the 3 Wonders located in the Americas. Select your favorite and tell why you chose it.

4 Which of the runners-up do you think most deserves to be one of the New 7 Wonders? Why?

5 Millions of people voted for the New Wonders. Why do you think the Wonders are important to so many people?